Years of Conflict

A Contradiction in Terms

Volume Three

Years of Conflict

William E. (Ted) Morris
International Poet Laureate of New Zealand

The Pentland Press Limited
Edinburgh · Cambridge · Durham

First published in 1993 by
The Pentland Press Ltd.
1 Hutton Close
South Church
Bishop Auckland
Durham

ISBN 1 85821 057 7

Typeset by Elite Typesetting Techniques, Southampton.
Printed and bound by Antony Rowe Ltd., Chippenham.

To my former loved wife Ruve who died 6th December, 1987 who was most supportive of my writing endeavours. As a professional proof reader she assisted with all of my 13 books published since 1953. She it was who said my major manuscript of 315 pages had to be published. This is the third of the four volumes, all of which I dedicate to her memory.

Of all literary forms poetry expresses man's deepest thoughts and feelings.

For the poet preserves, he feels, he creates, he hands on to posterity, and so becomes our history.

There is that which endures, the spirit of man, the flame of the poet.

The tragedy is that it takes a war – kill – or be killed to move men to the heights to write the finest verse, the most moving lines.

Poems written in war become treasure handed on from man's most wasteful occupation.

Lines taken out of context from part of the Dedication in what must have been the first book of poems published about World War II. Return to Oasis *by Victor Selwyn published by the Salamander Society, Cairo 1943.*

Contents

OTHER PUBLICATIONS BY William E. Morris

POETRY

Mission (War Poems)	England 1953
Silent Touches of Time	New Zealand 1971
Alchemy of Time	New Zealand 1975
Crucible	India 1981

PROSE AND POETRY

Te Awanui (Story of a War Canoe) N.Z.	1973
Waka Taua (second impression)	1975
Waka Taua (third impression)	1975
Good Thinking (in conjunction with J.H. Mitchell)	1976
Good Thinking (second impression)	1977
Treadmill of Time (completion of Trilogy)	1977
Zero's Children (International Year of the Child)	1987
A Contradiction in Terms (1st Vol. of 4)	1988
In The Beginning	1989
The Growing Up Years	1990

HISTORICAL

Journey Into Yesterday	1977
St. Peters 1879–1987 (A Centennial Publication)	1978

EDITORIAL

World Anthology (A Verse Mosaic By Living Poets)
One of four International Poets associated with compiling and editing this world publication on the death of its originator Dr. Orville Crowder Miller, and published by his widow Dorothy Munns Miller in America in 1980. 242 pp.

'The Coromandel Collection', painting and prose by Landscape Artist Da Vella Gore.
The prose text in her book shaped from her notes by myself. Published by Collins 1981.

The War Years

War is an exercise in futility
where people in high places
juggle with the lives of millions
and in that inept juggling
many of those millions die.

War has been waged in almost
every corner of our whirling globe
– except the Poles apart;
man's inhumanity to man has been
with us since the birth of Christ,
and the martyrdom of the Christians
by the Romans 2000 years ago.

It is ironic that in the crux of
Christendom the mouldering embers
of war stoked by warmongering nations
have flickered and flamed, burst into
war, died and burst again – the same
pattern embraces the Middle East today.

World War II and the wars that followed,
Korea and Vietnam, showed that civilians
died in almost the same ratio as the
soldier – it wasn't always the enemy
responsible;
war begins in the minds of men – peoples
of the world have come to believe that
wars are inevitable in the fabric of our
society – part of the tapestry of life;
as long as there are fanatics in the world
bemused with power and greed,
there could be wars; their
fanaticism is more dangerous than the nuclear
shadow;
The war years could be abolished if Man
changed his thinking to thoughts of Peace.

The Captured
Egypt, 1941

Barrage silk cast shadows where we sat on
kit bags, gas mask and tin hat embedded in
a crusted sand. We sat swatting Egypt's
flies with a peaked hat.
Our RTO was having someone on the mat,
still we sat, watching rusted prows of
sunken ships – grim reminder this was war,
a harbour bombed a little while before –
now Tewfik slumbered, as we reclined
uncomfortably on an alien shore.
Marching four abreast in column array
Hitler's beaten army halted for transport
in the bay, tired features creased by
particles of desert dust,
shabby uniforms infested by its all
embracing crust, dust entrenched
itself in ridges on headgear sadly worn,
irritated sweated forelocks closely shorn,
Down at heel boots made no imprint in sand
fringing polluted land – ugly born.

Bleak eyes had this sullen band
arrogant in their shifting sideways
stare, eyes that had witnessed swift
victory in other lands –
then reluctant surrender, chill despair,
a valedictory to high hopes
to triumph that was never really there.

Where shifting dunes shimmer under
Libya's molten sky
vultures cast shadows flying high over
rock-cairned graves where comrades lie.
'Neath windswept desert's rim barb wire
had hemmed them in;
between reaching fingers of twisted wire
threadbare prisoners* huddled as cattle
in a byre,
their hearts racked with questioning
doubt, minds seared from barb's reality.
Beings filled with but one desire,
to throw twigs on a home hearth fire.
Sentry go on sentry beat made mockery
of a dream complete –
they scrambled for the 'cigs' we threw
then cursed us 'cause there were so few.

**Italian prisoners of war.*

Toward Maadi

Straight converging rails shimmering in
beaten sun, sands warm to the touch;
train journey bisecting billowing dunes
past straggling mud abode villages –
electric units out of place at Maadi
station, gleaming pave past tented quarters
where English women dispense tea and cakes.

Maadi camp sprawling on dingy desert sand,
cluttering escarpment above Maadi village
where avenued jacarandas in purple bloom
led to stucco dwellings where ex-patriots
in diplomatic cosiness attempted to make a
corner of an English garden – entertained
big brass of the war, held tea parties at
four; one has a memory of me, a lowly gunner,
attempting to place reclining deck chair
right way up – beribboned officers of various
services who walked in high places watched
amusingly – my gracious host came to the
rescue; one came to know this family well.

Sort of people who made the effort to visit
when an operation saw you hospitalised for
some time – ward full of Americans, negroes
were there, veterans from operation 'Torch',
ward envied me such visitors; two charming
daughters accompanied their mother, smothered
me with kindness, a memory lingers to this
day of warmth of hospitality bestowed, when
one climbed steep stairs to a comfortable
abode.

Base camp for our New Zealand Division even had
an open air cinema where troops gathered row on
row and hurled derision at the screen if the show
was not to their liking, which was often, and no
amount of cajoling by the Manager would soften
their rage. Overall pattern of the base, saw a
sort of class distinction, not out of place,
officers rarely ventured among other ranks,
were sort of figureheads – no, more than that,
assumed an authority all their own, which in
their own minds was blown out of all proportion;
'Bludgers Hill' saw NCOs and O/Rs live in tents
together, one common bond all were graded unfit
for front line duty, either recovered from
severe battle wounds, illness, or physical
disability which only showed up in rigours of
desert campaigns – fate had decreed that one
should join this static breed.

Early evening air filled with concussion of
falling bombs not too far away – Italian
bomber seeming to float lazily in night sky
dropping its burden of destruction
indiscriminately – humble villagers would die.

One finally slept – woke to something amiss –
a world of stillness no sound penetrated,
voices didn't exist; both eardrums perforated
was verdict in Helwan hospital after a jolting
ride in ambulance; pain was intense week after
week, a vast stillness all around in a crowded
ward of skin graft patients – no other place
for me could be found.

Hospital overflowed when survivors of Greek
campaign lay in vast foyer, stretcher cases
row on row – bewilderment of defeat in their
eyes, dejection in a weary body, Navy risking
life and limb has rescued them from beach
heads littered with a repast of desperate
retreat.

Specialist on tour of duty restored my hearing,
said on discharge, 'On no account must you go
back to your artillery unit' – graded too unfit
for front line duty; one perhaps was fortunate
to be part of 'Bludgers Hill'; journalistic
experience with a typewriter spilled over into
recording casualties of war – sometimes into
early hours of morning, hurricane lamp flickering –
at my shoulder seeing in mind's eye each
phase of battle – how soldiers died in split
instant of machine gun's staccato chatter.

I Saw a Man Walking
Egypt, 1941

I saw a man walking, slowly, falteringly,
clotted blood coursed slowly so that limbs
were hesitant,
momentum was not of his volition
each step silent willing encouragement
gentle hands led him.
There was no gratitude in his eyes for
their sure support,
no lightening or quickening of a glance
in pleasure of needful aid from a trusted
helpmate.
Bandage and lint pressed close against
his forehead,
a compelled gaze could not see beyond to
sightless sockets.
Firm capable fingers rested lightly on each
side to guide him
for his hands were multiple wrappings
hiding charred stumps.

Doughy features blue-mapped with powder
burns
punctured with particles of infinitesimal
shattered steel.
A cataleptic walk insensible to dolour of
those who watched,
feeling behind an opaque wall the passageway
he must tread in slippered feet.
Yet, this was Man.
His garments loosely flapping about his
quiescent form.
A lath of skin and bone,
shroud of man wrapped in darkness,
shudderingly with shuffling steps he moves
across a shaft of sunlight – he would never
see.

The Sound and the Fury
Alamein, 1942

You crouched in a cacophonic world
where an orchestra of medieval hate
crashed out a symphony of discordant
note,
a chimera devoid of music;
quivering muzzles of guns purposefully
unfurled.
Terrain leaped and shuddered to sound,
sound battening itself on cotton-wooled
eardrums,
mouthed words lacerated in vibrant chaos,
vast all-embracing all-obliterating fury
flinging itself into battle.

Kaleidoscope of colours, of pink purple and yellows,
gun flashes as wadis erupt –
erupt into flame of rending fragmentation
tearing and mangling in frantic animation,
red hot metal screaming above bedlam,
crimson tongues licking heavens, dunes and desert
slashing enemy ramparts and mummified tree-trunks,
truncated branches beckoning in ghostly frenzy . . .
midst a reeling world.
Blasted face shocked into comprehending surprise
that death's searching fingers should reach so far,
emblazoned day turned into everlasting night.

Rubble Hill

A particular raid on Munich, October 1943

Eighteenth century baroque rococo
architecture
makes for a show piece that goes to
extremes –
churches like opera houses, and opera
houses like churches –
or so it seems.
Grandeur of Cavillies, backdrop for
glory, grossness, art and sin;
smell of incense from two hundred Catholic
institutions –
smells from beer, one hundred and three
million gallons
brewed each year.
In carousel, and in fun
where was memory of six million Jews –
killed by the Hun.

Largest university city of a
Federal Republic,
whose cobbled square
patterned millions of shuffling feet
mesmerised theatrically
by that Corporal's paranoid bleat.
Yet men who administered
the Final Solution in Eastern Europe
were avid connoisseurs of Mozart
in a city where politics and sport
are indissolubly imprinted in the heart.

Lavish ornate structures weathered
with age,
planned by the Court Dwarf
to Maximilian,
came tumbling down
one October night in '43,
in compelling beat
of combined heavy bomber's frown –
Pathfinders led the way,
let the bombers
have their block-busting sway.
They shovelled mortar, brick,
shattered limbs and smothered bodies
a thousandfold and more –
and built a rubble hill
from spill of futile war.

A Christian soul with loving care
shaped, with hands soft and white,
a small chapel
from broken brick and mortar –
a holy light,
perhaps in witness
to an inhuman night –
defied authority
when Olympic plans were laid,
continued to live
within the chapel he had made
while a monstrosity
of buildings cast shadows
where he walked –
looking down on the city that was
Munich.

Almost three decades
from carnage of the third Munich raid,
most lavish sixteen day production
the world has ever known, was staged.
Technologically perfect, computerised;
several years before
seeds had been sown on drawing boards,
slowly a concept grew,
life was breathed thereon,
steel and pylon were skeletal bones
metal and glass enduring flesh –
a skyline new beyond where
a new vociferous city grew;
acres of buildings
nurtured by urgent hands.

Amid this splendid sprawling
dome,
did one forget Dachau –
a *verboten* word to some –
was only eleven miles away.
How could there be peace
as doves flew high
into a cloudless sun flecked sky –
above a flickering
Olympic flame?
Thousands stood
before multi-coloured banners brave,
as athletes marched in slackly
serried ranks,
as jackbooted troops had –
was it thirty-four years before?
and after that came –
soul destroying bloody war.

What did $53,000,000 mean
when murder stalked amid life's stream?
Israeli athletes died
as no one stemmed that murder tide;
and all-strained most energy
of nations locked in sport –
was surely too dearly bought?
Munichen 'the home of the monks'
on gravel banks of the Isar,
built again
in quarter of a century's grace –
though blood was spilled
in another place –
on Rubble Hill.
Christian belief – perhaps
is locked there still –
on Rubble Hill?

"What did you do in the War, Daddy?"

If my eldest daughter at four had said,
'What did you do in the war, Daddy?' in all
honesty one would have to reply,
'Not much', yet circumstance decreed for me,
and me alone my spell of war away from a
true war zone – almost had its interesting
asides;
one gnawed on a bone of satisfaction in
different HQ units different vocations of work.

One knew Crete every stone, stick, tree,
and blade of grass on that beleagured
island – yet had never set foot upon it –
after evacuation one traced Maori war
dead on both Greece and Crete;
survivors only could tell me a true story;
laconically a Maori corporal would say
'Last I saw of Wiremu he was charging a
tank with an axe'; matter of fact
heroism blazed before your eyes of tales
told in battle fold.

Somehow after that one found oneself
liaison to Red Cross in Cairo,
interviewing men of Division who had
escaped from POW camps in Europe;
an interesting assignment was typist
to Junior Counsel for the defence in
a court martial – a Quartermaster
Sergeant on trial for living quite
beyond his soldier's pay – it went on
for a week or more – who won in the
end I can't be sure.

Then as one of three New Zealanders
representing the Division at Graves
Registration HQ Middle East, each
unit in the desert campaign through
Libya and into Tunisia now was
represented in this South African
command – my time there was brief,
with promotions of some consequence
due, one was recalled – a bitter pill
to digest – friendships made lasted
long after war's end now spaded back
into memory's fading page.
One was guilty of abusing an OC, he
listened quietly to my pent up fury
at having been brought back without
trial or jury – said 'I could have
you thrown in jail, instead I'm
sending you to Italy, have you any
objection to going?' One said 'No';
'You'll join Two Echelon above Taranto'.

After posting camp in desert outside
Alexandria in teeth of gale our small
convoy moved out – trip on small boat
was one of flying spume – and flying
vomit; visibility was nil, if we had
a navy escort we never knew; how one
suffered during those two and a half
days willing ship to stand still for
just one moment; at times it was
almost on its beam-end – Mediterranean
was going on such a bend.
Mount Etna thrust a plumed crest above
clouds – we went ashore in lighters –
it was almost Christmas Day, a war-torn
country lay ahead – maybe days of constant
dread.

Base camp a canvas town – a hustling
bustling place as primitive as gold
township of the eighties;
housed in tents we erected ourselves;
torrential rain forming channels of
racing water through our belongings –
cold and wet, icy wind of Appenines,
snow on its breath.
A *Casa*, once a German Headquarters
housed our Two Ec. 2 NZED unit.
One wing of upper structure a skeletal
frame where twenty-five pounders had pasted
again and again pushing enemy back
from toe of Italy – this was as
close as one had been to war – air
raids would herald it could be closer
still, spill of tension gnawing at
your stomach.

Imprint of War
Italy, 1943

Land desolate as a lone sheep lost from
flock in snowstorm's hazing; olive
trees walk as grey ghosts hand in hand,
denuded as sparse rock strata'd land;
land winter clutching at its throat,
manacled by invading armies steel
encircled moat.

A daub in artist's dingy scene child
figure tends a twig-fire green, sketchy
garments rent in every seam cling dejectedly
to a body honed to starvation's rampant paw;
misery oozes from his every being crouched
on feet ridged and raw, his legs as pea-
sticks after you had plucked pods – and left
sticks to weather's unruly nods; child body
pregnant in its import of need – all about
war's greed.
Wise eyes that stare apathetically through
an alien in narrow soul-destroying life
he always knew; across a curl of coiling
smoky haze a pleading cretin looks with
soul-filled gaze, hope tinged in thrust of
a wizened chin, an old man mask creased in
merest grin; embittered tread of war's
roughshod chariot, firmly imprinted on
features lineated in certain death.

Strident Strada

Polish armoured brigade moving up to Cassino

Cold *strada* welcomed a bleak dawn sun,
silver fortresses thundered from a
nocturnal run as an armoured brigade moved
up to a battleground that was Cassino;
there was an earthly stamp about them,
sweat glistened on hairless shiny domes,
dull unimaginative faces lacking the
twinkling eyes of gnomes;
thick pronounced features, sensuous lips,
stolid bodies girthed to the hips,
stocky soldiers strangely ill at ease,
far from a war-torn homeland trying hard
to please.
Infantrymen sat hunched 'neath lorry's
drab canvas hood,
there was bending room only,
no one could have stood;
at convoy length tires fled a swan song to
those days of dread, when tired feet in
hobnailed boots had tread
crumbling skin of blistered heels had bled.

Hanging their heads in peaceful mood,
their muzzles hooded
guns roll forward a menacing brood,
rude reluctant hosts lie supine,
tin hats tilted all awry,
gazing sombrely at a cotton ball sky;
Sherman tanks, squat, ungainly creatures
amble aimlessly
within the ranks of spaced and patterned
convoy file,
leeches of mosquitoes festooned themselves
on flesh
as mesh of caterpillar tread traced
its imprint in the pave with every mile;
tranquil features had these men never
fashioned for war's bewildering ken,
slow of mind as a slothful snail,
with crumbling soil of Italy ingrained
'neath broken fingernail – unknown
future twisted entrails with a torturing
fear; whole forenoon this convoy rumbled on,
tidy *strada* shuddered to its ceaseless beat –
then strangely conglomerate mass was gone –
those who had watched shivered in stifling
heat.

Strada: highway or road.
It was the Polish Brigade who breached the stalemate of Cassino.

Air Raid

Our HQ unit had just moved up to Bari,
settled down in what appeared to be an
empty warehouse, when banshee wailing of
air raid siren saw us stir uneasily in our
groundsheets – minds pleating a dread that
this was war.
Menacing drone of engines one even beat
then high pitched whine of falling stick
of bombs falling on and near the port – not
far away – crump of shell, crash of masonry,
crescendo of sound gathering momentum, coming
closer for a time; warehouse may have been target
for another air raid when ammunition ship was
blown to bits in harbour – on that day we heard
the bang – forty-seven miles away.

You could see sky through part of an arched beamed
roof, a few stars hard brilliant like diamonds
winked from small arc of sky – sound dragged down
through twisted trusses; drone grew fainter, silence
jarring ear-drums, no further sound of AA fire,
spent cartridge cases tinkling as they bounced on
empty streets into litter filled gutters.
We slept fitfully, ears cocked for that returning
drone, breakfast a cup of billy tea – we moved on
to Adriatic coast, moved and moved again amid
San Spirito's friendly village host.

Only air raids gave jarring essence that
this was war –
closer than you had ever been before to
its presence –
one bomb off target might spell it out for
you – enemy aerodromes were just across
Adriatic sea – it seemed a very narrow
reef-strewn stretch of water –
where village people, men, women and
children as nude as day they were born
(without appearing rude) splashed and
swam uncaring in a warm Italian sun;
undressed on beaches but you never saw
even a shapely leg using a sheet as
shelter before rushing helter-skelter to
rippling waters.

San Spirito

Thunder crashes in the hills
fork lightning slashes the sky,
down the narrow cobbled street
where fruit trees grow in circled
plots
raggle taggle children of the
village
swing straw covered carafes
in straggling line –
'tis the noonday hour and no
repast is complete without wine
on which to dine.

You wonder at the unafraidness of
the children
then realise that Europe's demarcation
line of seasons
has enveloped the Italian child all
his days,
wretched winter with its rain and mud,
rivers raging in full flood,
warm caressing golden sun of summer
tidal surge of Adriatic's sud.
And when you meet, silvery conversation
piece,
as hands do their best to speak.

A child – in no span of time a woman
barely in her teens;
fecund earth enmeshes itself within a
framework of Italian life,
a family spills over in the selfsame façade
behind selfsame front doors.
Children laugh, show even white teeth –
and somewhere in the distance not too
far away planes drop bombs.
Italian's child has lived in poverty
all its days,
and lived through wars in which it had no say.

B 25 Strike

Mostly we saw them as a silver pencil thread
cross-stitching an arc of sky, nudging clouds
on their mission of death and destruction
to know targets across the Adriatic Sea;
American air bases of some magnitude camouflaged
themselves across miles of country in toe of Italy;
All this might went on display one day
when B 25s struck at oil-fields across way
somewhere in belly of Europe; heavens throbbed
to massive V formations wave on wave, we watched
them out of sight – and saw them return, not
neat echelons that were there before – stragglers
trailing smoke, flying low, and one just knew
that there were gaps that didn't show;
mission accomplished – oil-fields out of commission
for a long while – memorial to the young American
dream, boys who had seen little of war who died
in blazing bombers – even before they'd emptied a
bomb bay – died in a pitiless holocaust of flame
their bodies just a charred remain.

Italian Scene

Sometimes it is a grey world
gnarled trunks of olive trees
march in close column over rolling
upland; patterned fields rise to
far-flung horizon with here and there
a fresh strip of light loam soil
furrowed behind ancient plough;
in distance, swatched in blue mists
rugged mountain peaks thrust jagged
snow-capped crests to a sullen sky.
There are days when whole world
is enveloped in greyness, fitful
gusts of sleet and hail, blanketing
rain falling ceaselessly; when atmosphere
is brittle with harshness of winter,
wind from Apennines forces spoken words
back in the throat – ice on its breath.
Hemmed in by an avenue of low stone wall
on either side,
highway gathers beauty unto itself
in its tidy order of giant thumbstones
at spaced intervals;
clean cut black and white culverts of
diagonal line bridging dried water
courses.

There is no bush, as we know it, no stream
no river in toe of Italy, just undulating
countryside, whitewashed squared edifices
which go to form a village huddled together
clinging precariously to a prominent peak
to look from a distance for all the world
as a turreted castle;
stony terraces sparsely cultivated remind
one very much of Valley of Wilderness, close
to gleaming rails on uplifting way to Jerusalem.
Curving through valley cross-pieced telephone
wires give an image of a triple set of pearl
buttons on a woman's blouse – and thoughts
turn momentarily from peasant countryside of
southern Italy to home far far across blue
Mediterranean.
Overhead mighty four-engined fortresses thunder
while twin-tailed fighter planes flaunt
lanes from dawn to dusk; to bring
us back from a reverie that this is war.

There are days when the sun shines on
clustered villas with boundaries of crumbling
stone walls; on quaint thatch-like grain sheds
in rambling yard of a peasant farm;
black-ribboned highway winds itself uphill
and down dale – its length resounding to
roar of fast moving convoys – a conglomeration
of mobility into battle – up there on the
Sangro river.

Goodbye Italy

Reclining back on officer's luggage in an
open truck
air filled with derisive remarks from friends
marching to the port –
one gazed reflectively at pristine whiteness
of two chevrons on left sleeve of service
shirt –
hard to believe that after exactly four years
overseas that they were there;
memories raced across the mind of hosts who
had been so very kind in that Italian village
left behind; Giovanni, a tailor who did his
work with pride,
a few packets of army issue cigarettes
satisfied,
neat pressed shirts, and shorts made in a
'twinkling of an eye'; once we visited his
home, looked aghast at small raw octopi upon
a plate each feeler spread green leaf
vegetable in between; turned it this
way and that,
tentatively cut into a feeler –
his wife with a brood of children at
her skirts deftly took our plates
away – fried eggs on a platter saved
the day – we sampled bottles of wine
forming a centrepiece on white scrubbed
deal table – drank as much as we were
able.

Beyond a boundary fence at foot of
garden of our HQ
a beautiful Italian woman dwelt,
her husband was a stationmaster
somewhere further north –
he never seemed to be at home,
she seemed to thrive on being alone –
she was no courtesan.
Her table, when we got to sit at it,
infrequently,
was mahogany covered with heavy cream
lace, silvery cutlery, fine wines,
exquisite liqueurs, and gourmet dishes
on which to dine, to halted English
conversation, in elegant surroundings –
we called her 'the stationmaster's
lady', who knew her by no other name;
in some respects she seemed so out
of place when war had placed its
frown on this Italian town, poverty
predominated everywhere –
starvation with its ugly stare.
Yet one will always remember hospitality
shared,
and we in turn would arrive shirts bulging –
chocolate for the children –
tinned goods for the table,
cigarettes for menfolk saved from issue –
one didn't smoke,
colleagues came to me when they were
broke;
yoke of poverty ceased a little now and then,
because of our presence among this village ken.

We learnt the language, that is some of us did,
voluble hands and tongue together –
one still waves hands about when talking;
how easy it was to learn Italian, a soft
silvery language delightful to the ear,
expressive too, each word so right once
its meaning had been made clear;
friendships grew more readily with no
language barrier,
how important language is to understanding
of nations,
no longer a 'poor relation' on the outside
looking in, so comfortable in this new
found skin.
Aroused from this reverie there was the
port, and at the wharf a Blue Star liner
pride of the fleet – *Arundel Castle* –
to greet me and those converging feet
still coming – marching loosely with
carefree mein – the war for them was over –
only a very few, the very fit would see
Italy again.
For all, life would never be the same –
the pity of war – from boyhood to manhood
in almost five years – years lost –
at what cost.

Going Home

Swinging on a derrick over Alexandria harbour
officer's luggage in a sling beneath my feet,
ears still concussed from depth charges, as
navy made room to lower boom on German submarine
waiting at harbour entrance for our large
troopship to zoom into periscope view; what a
bedlam, one minute cruising serenely, the next
navy making vast sweeps, waves curving from
bow, searching keenly for sonic sound,
shipboard a little apprehension growing; no oil
slicks that we knew licked bosom of Mediterranean
sea, which had behaved most decorously on our
short journey from Italy.

Thoughts churned looking from on high at
this ancient seaside resort,
of an evening stumbling through its
streets in total blackout,
several years before,
when Rommel was just out there with
his armoured might – thus there could not
be one glimmer of light – a city shrouded
in darkness; tyres sung a song of going
home, a burdened convoy heading south,
past Cairo with its hungry mouth,
Maadi village, Maadi camp where we would
languish for a while –
and lose our home vision smile.

We slept on groundsheets alongside our
empty truck, in a sense we were veterans
of war – desert sands might grow cold, to
us the night was balmy, we slept under
galaxy's arcing fold, stars hung like
milky opals in the sky, as a large melon-
coloured moon slowly drifted by.

Image in Passing

Cairo, 1944

Conclave of brittle grained splayed feet
had slapped stone smooth; stone which patterned
steps and stairs emerging into corridors
behind which usurers in grubby galabiahs
rubbed greasy palms – for them no cry of 'bucksheesh'
for alms;
treading carefully with upward gaze
a grotesque object you pass enveloped in a
bloated carcase, bowed beneath weight of precious
liquid in its skin-fold; a lifelike beast
with four protruding legs slung as a halter;
somnolent volition of crab-wise shambling movement,
an old man living a lifetime of perdition
rubbing sharded shoulders against age old structure.

He could not see compassion in my glance,
rhuemy eyeballs glued to knees;
he went sideways on the stair,
an abject being not seeing it was you
not he who contaminated his path –
usurper on his well-trod measure of
yesterdays;
did he as he edged away mutter into a
neglected bedraggled beard 'Allah be praised'?
Lowly though it be, at least I have a job –
a litany of prayer his burden lightened
on a downward stair.

You passed but once in his faltering path
in an alien war torn land, where children
with fly diseased eyes live a little then
die on Cairo's mottled strand – die without
a whimper, or a cry – lie on scrabbled footways
where they die;
water boys plod upstairs and down in endless
enduring days, bewildered if someone should
fling a word of praise into a plethora of a
daily task, a crucible which squeezes and shrivels
into a selfsame obliterating mask.

Journey Towards Home

Month after month went by at Maadi Camp
as if someone had taken time by the forelock
and everything was standing still – not so in
the Orderly Room of which one was in charge,
too busy to even ask for leave to buy farewell
presents for family and friends close at hand;
rumours spread and rumours died, July to September
we wondered when rumours would become reality –
sighed for home, we'd had enough of desert sand,
and unreal living.

A tub of a ship to make journey from Tewfik
to Bombay, coaling at Aden on the way;
lighters tugged to ship's side laden with
slack coal,
chocolate loin-clothed bodies as a train of
ants forming a human chain, sweat stained
stringy muscles gleaming in blazing sun;
all day long they shovelled coal (possibly
for a mere pittance), no halt in that human
endeavour for a midday meal – or cooling
shower, from early morn to late evening they
toiled perpetual motion, dehumanization;
hills seemed to thrust township into harbour
rising perpendicularly from the streets –
cylindrical reservoir caught morning sun,
and on a steep twisting path people walked,
we envied them what cool there was teasing
their faces; we sweltered in hottest harbour
on earth, as we endured Aden's heated sultry
breath.

Going back thousands of years it is known
that Cleopatra had built on these
inhospitable heights several wells; there
were faint traces of ancient aqueducts,
crumbling walls of stone against grey shale.
We came into Bombay harbour in late evening,
there was no blackout, the long line of
waterfront glowed with lights from buildings
large and small, tall façade of Taj Mahal
Hotel was a fairyland with its cluster of
twinkling coloured fluorescent against
spared battlements, as if they had been
coloured pebbles picked in handfuls, and
flung at random to form a beaded slate.

Our passenger list already swelled by Yank
airmen who had flown over the 'Hump' in the
Burma campaign, was swelled again when Polish
refugees bound for our country waiting in a
transit camp many many months; long arm of
coincidence was here, a US sailor heard from
his childless wife she was adopting two
children among Polish refugees, he looked up
the embarkation list, and was overjoyed to
find his children there; strange, wasn't it,
that in the first place the sailor should be
on that ship; that his adopted children
should be in the first batch of refugees,
and they should meet halfway across the
world on the pulsating deck of an armed
merchantman – who says life isn't patterned
for we humans on this earth?

They were young children, the first batch
to come aboard, fragile youngsters neatly
and cleanly clad for they had been in European
hands a long while waiting this day; some
with bonnets, many without, fair hair flat on
the forehead framing fairer features,
brother clinging to sister assisted up that
long gangplank by US doughboys, who were
enjoying the novelty; reluctant to let go
of their worldly possessions, clutching them
tightly to puny chests, as they stepped
manfully forward down that long corridor,
to where we waited to feed them milk and
hot bread; watch them take those berth
tickets, here is a pretty girl of some four
years, life is a joke, see that smile
impudent unafraid, she takes her ticket as
if it really belonged to her in the first
place; older girls were big and sturdy with
sad expressions in tired eyes – they were
remembering loved eyes they would never see
again – they were old enough to remember,
holocaust of the Warsaw Ghetto.
Some were dressed in uniforms not unlike
Girl Guides with Polish shoulder flashes,
natty beret sat sitting over shiny tresses;
some wore shoes too large, and frocks too
small, all were stockingless; there were
a few older folk guided by stiff starched
nurses who rustled when they walked
alongside their charges – red cross gleaming
brazenly against the white.

There were old, old women with straggly grey
hair, bowed shoulders dressed in faded
out granny cottons; their children would
have been much older than those about them;
perhaps careworn features in a sunken face
were apathetic to the solicitude extended
to them.

They had seen and suffered much, hearts
were shattered under that shabby exterior –
still there was the will to live come
what may; there were no menfolk, boys in
their early teens with fearless features,
frank and open mein eager for the adventure,
making friends quickly with members of the
crew who spoke their language – it was a
pity there was not more of them to become
future citizens of New Zealand. There were
seven hundred of them, only a few destined for the USA.

The Ship

'Smoking out lamps on port side!'
how strange to hear a cry used
by merchant sailors through the
centuries – as old as the navy itself,
in a year of 1944 in the Indian Ocean
coming home from war.

Her camouflaged sides gave her the
appearance of a cruiser, especially
a purposeful armament of fifty-four, including
four five inch guns; there were 19,000
tonnes of her, length 184 metres, cruising
speed 20 knots; alongside, as if cloned,
her sister ship honed to same sharp awareness
of conflict, both Liberty ships churned
from a Kayser shipyard Stateside, two
whose keels may have lain side by side;
her crew, 400 including marines for shore
duty – we NZers numbered 1810, there were
a few Australians, and Chinese airforce
officers – and cadets bound for America –
the war hadn't touched them, yet; how
effeminate they were, clean and starched
at all times – never unbending, lending
an air of unreality to a troopship, one
General George Randall V, her sister
General George Mitchell – both immobile
at anchor swinging gently to a slack tide
down which they would ride forging a bow
trail through a buoyed Bombay harbour.

Our ship had seen action in the Solomons –
a stretcher below decks recorded in stark
bold letters a small list of killed, and
wounded – a reminder that the war we
thought we had left behind was still
with us today – and maybe, just maybe,
out in that long stretch of ocean a
submarine lurked – waiting.

American Allies

How different to the soft spoken New England
Americans one had worked with at Heliopolis,
these had seen thirty-three months of service
overseas – airforce crews who had witnessed
action in the Western Desert, Tripoli, and
Tunisia, Pantelleria in Sicily, and Foggia
in Italy, and some who had flown over the
'Hump' in the Burma campaign; it has been a
hard apprenticeship leaving scars on body
and mind – memories of comrades left behind.
On ship slacks cut ragged to the knees,
faces with a profuse hirsute growth,
upper lip running riot – or just a five
o'clock shadow permanently there;
what a contrast to those soldiers from
the States, we saw in thousands in Cairo
in 1943, clean shaven, clothes tailored
skin tight, slacks creased (never shorts)
shirt sleeves always buttoned at the cuff –
many of them died on an Anzio beachhead.

Our Americans played poker for chips,
and Banco, others liked to talk, tall
with brooding eyes, of days that had been;
spoke of super flying fortresses on a
secluded airfield near Calcutta, bristling
with armament, verily a fortress, its
vast wingspread halving the fuselage, and
high in the cloud lanes as Canadian geese
in V formation nosing heavens to a known
destination. With bitterness in their
voices they tell of sacrificing speed
for a higher ratio of strike power – there
is longing in their voices when they
mention Mosquito and Mustang in those
early days of an american war after Pearl
Harbour – the former they swore – ace of
bombers.
Affectionately we dubbed them 'God darned
cock suckers', don't ask me why, these boys
who fly are made of sterner stuff than army
doughboys who in the past had played their
war as gridiron football – you want something
more than brawn muscle and ballyhoo –
when flak is like a curtain of steel – spelling
death in every concussed breath.

Reflections on the Equator

Imaginary line around the earth
90 degrees distant from the poles
at all points – divides earth into
North and South hemispheres;
it is there, once Crossing the Line
was enacted with ceremonial *élan* –
we crossed Equator at 11.30 am on
October 17 – it was not my plan to
be having a haircut – but I was, a
clumsy ritual of the Line in a not too
distant age and clime.
The Americans aboard will tell you
they cross the Equator Line twice –
once in the Indian Ocean, once in the
Pacific, by the time they step on home soil
they will have crossed the Equator four
times.
Reflecting in like terms, we NZers have
experienced six summers in four years;
Americans talk wistfully of snow and
bob-sledding ice, and ice skating, from
humid heat of a stinking jungle they step
into crisp clean cold air of a Fall season –
we have no reason to be jealous of them.

For me a green sward, white figures
running between wickets, cricket and all
its attendant joys;
Summer with fields a carpet of clover,
red rata blooming high in virgin forest
in December, and the Christmas flower,
snow white clematis, pristine stars
sprinkled amid green foliage;
rippling green clear fold of boulder
strewn mountain stream;
conjured memory a reality two weeks
sailing away – give a day – who knows
what may be in our way?

Just Reflections

I'm reminded of Whittaker's poem:
White waves heaving high my boys –
and white waves heaving high – for
days now a gale has been cutting our
bow, leaning over the rail, spray has
leapt into the face;
waves do not break, they spread themselves
as foam in a washtub, and in their spreading
remind one of coloured glass so translucent
are the seething waters, a shimmering blue
changing to filmy green, then just a narrow
flange leaving a trail to the horizon, as
if a huge whale, or a sinister sub was about
to push its slim periscope and lean baleful
being to the surface – each day horizon is
there, you might bisect an ocean – but one
never reaches an horizon, it truly tilts
itself over the edge of the world.

This morning we buried the dead, to remind
us that in life death is sometimes only a
step away; there had been no action, and
'we' literally translated meant the personnel
of the ship – for a marine had taken his
life;
Beyond the laconic statement over the PA
system 'all hands bury the dead' we passengers
allowed only our minds to dwell topside,
envisaging the ceremony on portside of weather
deck – the storm was still with us.
There was no fuss, not even a farewell salute
that I remember; it was over very quickly,
and the remains of one Thomas J. Murphy of US
Marine Corps slid to the depths of the Indian
Ocean a long long way down – not even a
wreath floated on the turbulent waves to mark
his spirit's going.

More Reflections

Our sister ship mostly lagged behind in
the Australian Bight, the New Zealand
Navy made a kind gesture coming between
us to say 'farewell' – we were on our
own – the way ahead was safe – and known.
We had come past Cape Luon off Albany
southernmost point of Western Australia,
now our troopship was south, far south,
the westering sun goes down on our blunt
end, as we bend back toward Melbourne;
skies are grey and deck plates wet from
chilly rain.

Days ago one was grumbling of the heat,
combating the cold, slacks and jerseys
are worn – and some there were in greatcoats
as well; our vessel rolls to a
long surging cross swell so that sometimes
one could almost see down the funnel
of the *George Mitchell*;
two thousand miles from home, four days
sailing day and night, how slow the days
go, walking to and fro from mess to
hammock through narrow space of corridors
slanting to the swell from port to starboard
and slowly recovers, to repeat
the performance over again, we had become
used to it and kept our feet from the
Bass Strait slough.

Yesterday there was gunnery practice, the
ship shuddered and shook to the curious
clang-like resound as big five inch shells
pumped forth for a time; it was a different
chime when the bracket of bofors added a
staccato overture to the crescendo – target
for big guns was difficult to hit in an up
and down world of ocean.
American style eating is a meal at 7 am
and another at 4 pm; one begins to tire
of 'cawfee' instead of tea, spamburgers in
place of meat, jelly instead of a milk
pudding, and ice cream – an endless supply,
fresh meat would come aboard at Port Melbourne
if latrine rumours didn't lie.

Storm

It is a grey day horizon circles our bow
in a white foam of rolling wave;
a heaving sea of greenish hue engulfing
our sister ship so that one moment she is
plunging to her plimsoll line (if she had
one) and next riding on a crash of turbulent water rolling horribly, with a stern
making valiant efforts not be smothered
in that wall of sea.
Our transport's sharp prow cleaved spray
to the top deck, ocean swell seems to be
but a hand's throw from rail, deck slants
so that one walks as if breasting a strong
wind clutching grimly to any handhold;
fine spray has made a slippery foothold,
from a force ten gale; on our starboard
side gale lashes an empty deck except for
a lone sentry huddled under forward staircase,
some shelter from the searching storm.

Port Melbourne

Port Melbourne was a quiet backwash in a
noon hour HMS *Adelaide* berthed close to a
cement pier.
It is a new scene, there are patched hills on
our starboard side as we come into a horseshoe
harbour, towns and villages dotted on either
side, green trees, architecture in southern
hemisphere style, smoke curling from chimney
stacks – tide is slack, ship moves slowly
as if in convoy pack;
clean white cumulus cloud rolls on crests
of low undulating hills, an island spills
itself against our port side, a chain of
rock-linking mainland; habitations become
more clustered spires of a city pointing
themselves between high stacks of factories
belching forth smoke on a severely drab
waterfront.
A Naval dockyard where corvettes in a state
of brown unreadiness behind barriers of
scaffolding were being built – maybe the war
would be over before sea readiness; our
sister ship berthed slowly on our portside;
long lines of Red Cross cars and buses
were soon filled, we said 'goodbye' to
Australian Air Force personnel, and some
NZers whose homes were in this beautiful
city on the Yarra; heavy luggage was left
behind – a working party soon whisked this
away.

Dominating the whole scene were women's
services in khaki and airforce blue who
looked after their passengers with crisp
efficiency.
For me the wharf of Melbourne under my feet
as NCO in charge of loading chilled beef onto
our troopship; blood thinned by a central
Mediterranean sun cool breeze from Yarra's
placid waters had a bite to it – one was glad
to get aboard again – two lorries of muslin
covered beef of 147lb quarters had been loaded
in quick time – fresh meat on board – goodbye
to American spam, and everything else that
came out of a can.

Another port, another day, once more we are on
our way going through Bass Strait lone lighthouse
blinking a friendly beam to keep you from waters
which were not what they seem;
close on our starboard side a smooth faced rock
worn by wind and wave looked for all the world
as a boat bottom upwards, shorn of its blunt end –
seabirds cluttered its smooth crest;
a lone plane circled, we were in the Tasman Sea
rolling to a heavy swell, which bumped us more
as night wore on;
one more day we should berth in Wellington harbour
home sweet home – more or less, at least a blessed
arbour from tensions of war.

The Tasman

Sun has been shining, Tasman is like a
sulphur flow down a volcanic cone, an
oily swell capped by turbulent tempests
of white foam eddying as breaking waves
on a seashore;
withal it is a brittle waterway, in spite
of sun's rays one instinctively knows that
scudding wake below the hawser chain is cold,
involuntarily one scans the limitless sea
to a foam-tossed horizon for even smallest of
ice floes – once again we are far south;
only bulge in panorama is heaving swell –
boat deck slants to 45 degrees as ship wallows
in Tasman's trough;
one is counting the hours now, dawn tomorrow
should see us turning north sun on our blunt
end bending toward a friendly coast.

Home

We came up from the south into Wellington heads
with a cold blustery wind whipping off the
Kaikouras snow-capped from unseasonal snow –
the Straits only a gentle swell, fishing boats
cruising beyond buoyed nets in the channel,
and the clean breeze being breathed in deeply
by one and all – after confines of a troopship
it was sweet beyond recall.

Our Yankee trooper anchored in mid-stream
looking for one moment as if she might
beach on the girdled foreshore at Petone
across the harbour, giving us a grand view
of Soames Island – after the official
inspection we came quietly in to berth;
first message over the tannoy from our
Minister of Defence was to tell us we were
no longer furlough troops, the doubt of
return in our minds removed – it was a
fantastic welcoming home present; did
that Air Force band on the wharf sound the
better because of that, or did Wellington
looking all huddled up as if it had shrunk
since we saw it last – wrapped in a solemn
calm, did that speak 'home' to some of us,
or was it those lucky blighters who had
loved ones waiting behind the barrier,
which set your eyes glistening, or the
thought that in that other island someone
might greet you as lovingly – or would they?

First class accommodation on a well known
island ferry; Wellington looking like a
cavern lit by glow worms dim blackout just
piercing evening haze from the hills;
ghost-like figures silhouetted against dark
buildings, screw revolving more quickly as we
slid away from the ferry wharf.
Tea where one sat down to sheer white tablecloths
and fine china cups and saucers, waited upon
instead of fending for oneself – later, clean
sheets in a four berth cabin – our passage
down the coast smooth – so smooth as if the
ship was moving in a well oiled groove.

Another band, a more enthusiastic crowd, a
first class carriage, parks and a meandering
river, a well loved Cathedral city bathed in
brilliant sunshine – memories crowded of that
year of 1938-39, joyous memories of city life
always with its minimal strife;
breakfast at the station, lunch and dinner at
a service club; the hours ticked by and in the
early hours of the morning we boarded a rail-car
whose bogey wheels said 'Going home, Going home' –
rail-car halts at a dear familiar station crowded
with well-wishers; loved ones were there your
brother and his wife, you're back in the family
fold; war a long way behind – and you don't
have to go back ever.
Relax 'fella' you can wallow as a lotus eater
in the courts of idleness amidst prevalent
rain on our wet West Coast there will be sunshine –
lest one forgets those Egypt days, and Italian
skies in an unreal world where you were on stage
for a time, in an unreal play – now you have
pulled the curtain down forever.